# AN INCREDIBLE INDIAN

# AN INCREDIBLE INDIAN

by

## Dan L. Thrapp

Texas
Western
Press

THE UNIVERSITY OF TEXAS AT EL PASO

SOUTHWESTERN STUDIES No. 39

Second Edition
ISBN 87404-193-7

 All Texas Western Press books are printed on acid-
free paper.

# FOREWORD

It has been almost 20 years since this biographical work on Juh, one of the remarkable Apache war leaders of history, was first published. In the intervening period there have surfaced a couple of instances where clarification is indicated.

A fine biography of Geronimo appeared in 1976, written by an esteemed historian, the late Angie Debo, whose integrity, impeccable research and superb writing skills are everywhere recognized. In that book however, she unaccountably, as it seems to me, wrote Juh completely out of a most spectacular feat of arms: the 1882 extraction at gunpoint of several hundred individuals from the San Carlos Reservation of Arizona, and herding them south to Mexico through country thickly coursed by U.S. Army detachments. I believe, on the other hand, that Juh was he who conceived, led and directed this notable émeute and that Geronimo was his subordinate, as explained in the accompanying biography. Angie Debo informed me that she had so written almost entirely because Jason Betzinez, who was one of those taken from San Carlos in that adventure, had not mentioned Juh in his narrative, *I Fought With Geronimo*. That is true. He did not.

It must be remembered that this was not a tight group of warriors who performed the feat. The Apaches did not operate like cavalry. The raiding party consisted of groupings, each under its own leader, operating independently while more or less committed to a common

{ i }

goal. It is possible that Betzinez did not accompany the portion led by Juh, or think to mention him because he was concerned with his own relationship to Geronimo.

If Geronimo *did* accomplish this miracle it was the most stupendous event of a life not noted for anything else remotely of such caliber. Only Juh had the military genius to plan and carry out this sensational feat. In addition, evidence placing Juh in the leading role is overwhelming: The American consul at Chihuahua reported Juh was at Casas Grandes where the raid was organized, and was determined to lead it. Colonel Mackenzie's reliable spy at Corralitos reported that "Ju, apache chief, here. Think will go for San Carlos..." S. D. Pangborn, acting agent at San Carlos, reported "there is good reason to believe that Juh himself was here." Colonel Orlando Willcox, commanding the Department of Arizona, reported that "Juh and Geronimo" were leading the raiders. Captain Alexander MacGowan, a reliable and well informed officer, said the hostile, Natiotish "met Hoo... near Eagle Creek... This information can be relied upon." Ace Daklugie, Juh's son, said Juh led the raid. General George Crook wrote that "ju and Hieronymo" were the leaders.

And there is still more persuasive evidence. In all of Geronimo's career there is no parallel for the stunning operation, nothing to demonstrate he had the imagination, the capacity or followers enough to carry it out.

With Juh, however there *is* an exact parallel, as this biography illustrates: in 1879 when the hard-pressed Victorio was trying to escape into Mexico from the Black Range with his people, Juh stormed to his assistance. Juh-led warriors rushed up from Mexico, slammed into the ranches and communities along the Rio Grande and created such confusion and panic among whites that Victorio could save himself and all his followers.

Juh was the *one* strategist and supreme tactician among latter-day Apaches, and he was the master-mind who led the great breakout, an awesome feat, indeed.

In another instance this biography states that Juh

and Geronimo led some of their people into Mexico on the 1876 breakup of the Chiricahua Reservation, and has little to report of their activities for the next several years. Further study shows that this is what occurred: Arizona Governor Anson P.K. Safford learned, probably from the acting governor of Sonora, Vicente Mariscal, with whom he was in touch, that the Apaches who had fled into that state under Juh numbered 208, and that they had been led by the white renegade, Zebina Streeter (see my *Encyclopedia of Frontier Biography* for the Streeter story). Streeter had been an officer in the Juárez forces which defeated Maximilian and, as such, claimed also membership in the American Legion of Honor which would entitle him to honorary Mexican citizenship. He and Mariscal had been involved in the climactic battle against the French emperor of Mexico and doubtless were acquainted, perhaps were friends. Now Streeter interceded with Mariscal, as is supposed, and persuaded the Sonora official to grant Juh, Geronimo and their people asylum in Sonora so long as they behaved themselves and committed no depredations, a peace policy to which they adhered for three or four years. That appears to be why Juh was permitted to remain peacefully in Mexico, and did so until the Victorio turbulence coaxed him north once more.

As this biography makes clear, Juh was a complex, important man in frontier history. It is to be hoped that a still more complete account of his life may some day appear.

DAN L. THRAPP
Tucson, Arizona
November, 1991

Ace (Asa) Daklugie, son of Juh, taken in 1910. This man was said to bear a strong resemblance to his father, of whom no photograph is known to exist.

JUH, BY AGE AND WARLIKE SPIRIT a contemporary of Victorio, was in all respects save appearance the epitome of the Apache warrior. His name is sprinkled through military dispatches and reports of hostilities and depredations during the nineteenth century, though a coherent account of his life never has appeared in print, nor was he well known to whites during his own lifetime. Yet Juh was a prominent and important Apache, of singular capacity and ruthlessness, deserving to rank with Cochise, Mangas Coloradas, Victorio and well above Geronimo in accomplishment. He was little known largely because of personality traits that made his career difficult to trace at the time and to recover later. One reason he was so imperfectly known was that he was an individualist, too haughty to attract or to retain large numbers of followers, except on rare occasions and so, despite his undoubted ability, he never had quite the impact that his illustrious colleagues possessed. Much of his activity was confined to Old Mexico; therefore, his fame north of the border rests largely upon incidents sporadic in nature, but spectacular in effect.

Juh, whose name usually was pronounced like a rather explosive "who," was born in the 1820s, virtually at the same time as Victorio. He was son of a leading man of the Nednai (Netendia, Netdahe, Nednhi) band of Southern Chiricahuas,[1] and saw the light of day prob- ably in Sonora. The Southern Chiricahuas, whose own name for themselves approached Deindai,[2] or "enemy people," appear to have possessed an unsavory reputation even among some of their relatives. Betzinez reports that "they were outlaws recruited from other bands, and included in their membership a few Navajoes as well as Mexicans and whites who had been captured while children and who had grown up as savages. We Warm Springs [Mimbres] Apaches regarded the Netdahe as being true wild men, whose mode of life was quite different from that of the reservation Indians, being devoted entirely to warfare and raiding the settlements."[3]

Juh "is a bad Indian," Colonel Orlando Bolivar Willcox, commander of the military Department of Arizona, conceded, "and is constantly raiding and creating disturbances,"[4] an assessment which was widely held.

## Origin of His Name

John Rope said his Apache name was *Tanbinbilnojui*, meaning He Brings Many Things With Him, attesting to his skill as a raider.[5] The name Juh may derive from the last syllable of his soubriquet. Spelling variants range through Ju, Ho, Whoa, Hoo, and anything else to put in writing the fact that the name was pronounced by Chiricahuas themselves as "hon," with just a trace of the final "n".[6] "If Ju (or Juh)... would kindly inform the press how he spells his name, he would have the satisfaction of knowing that when he dies on the field of glory, he would not be orthographically mangled in the dispatches," grumbled a reporter for the *Daily Alta Californian.*[7]

According to Betzinez and Griswold, Juh's name meant "long neck," but a Chiricahua, Samuel E. Kenoi, told the ethnologist, Morris E. Opler, that Juh's name "doesn't mean anything. He was called that because he stuttered." He considered him a "war shaman," and Opler adds that Juh "has been consistently described as aggressive and cruel."[8] He became chief of the Nednai as a young man, and continued in that capacity until his death, about age 60 in 1883.

Before his teens, his parents took him north to visit the Bedonkohe Apaches near present-day Clifton, Arizona, where he was found by Jason Betzinez to reveal a

playful, if mischievous, character.[9] A decade later, in the 1840S, he returned to the Bedonkohes and married Ish-keh, a granddaughter of the noted chief, Mahko, and a first cousin of Geronimo,[10] thus establishing a connection with the
Apache with whom he would live, raid and depredate almost until his death. He resided with his wife's people for a number of years, then took her back to his own band, south of the border.

## His Rise to Leadership

Juh must have completed his warrior's training (more formalized in Apache society than one would suppose[11]) with a great deal of enthusiasm, for he became one of the most outstanding practitioners of the arts of raiding and ambuscade, armed clashes and skirmishes in the history of white-Apache relationships. In an 1855 battle between the Apaches and Mexicans near Namiquipa, on the upper Santa Maria River, one hundred miles northwest of Chihuahua City, Juh, then about 30, is said to have demonstrated through his outstanding leadership that he was a fit candidate for the chieftainship. Betzinez said that "the fight was a severe one but because of Juh's brilliant leadership resulted in a victory for the Apaches."[12] The Southern Chiricahuas appeared to concentrate their marauding in the border country near the Chihuahua-Sonora line and in southwestern New Mexico and southeastern Arizona. Casas Grandes,[13] an historic town in extreme western Chihuahua, one hundred twenty-five miles southwest of El Paso, seems to have been the settlement to which they were most attracted, in whose vicinity they frequently were reported, and near which Juh died.

## His Physical Appearance

Juh was not a typical Apache in appearance, for he was tall and heavy, according to most reports. Charles F.

This watercolor was made from life by Mrs. Mary P. G. Devereux in January, 1881, at the subagency near Fort Thomas. Differences have been voiced over whether it is an accurate likeness. *(Photo Courtesy Arizona Historical Society)*

Lummis, war correspondent of the *Los Angeles Times*, reported in 1886 that he had been "one of the most dangerous Apaches," erroneously thought him about 36 or 37 at his death, and said he was "nearly six feet tall in his moccasins, very dark skinned, and had an impediment in his speech. He was a hard, merciless savage of great determination and a terror all along the border."[14] Cruse reported that "Juh was a very fat Indian—something unusual among Apaches. He weighed at least two hundred and twenty-five pounds."[15] James Kaywaykla, an Apache who as a child knew the chief well, said that he was "a powerful figure," who towered over Nana, himself described as close to six feet tall. Juh "was very large, not fat, but stockily built. His body was twice as thick" as Nana's. "His heavy hair was braided and the ends fell almost to his knees. His features... were what people now call Mongoloid."[16] It would seem that, if Juh was as active and as tall as Kaywaykla recalled, the weight Cruse gave him would not necessarily prove him to be "fat." Whether fat or stocky, Juh was a leader of fighting men. The fact that he held the chieftainship of a particularly warlike band of Apaches for more than thirty years attests to that. Betzinez said Juh was "a good leader," that he was "highly capable," and that he was "particularly liked" by his band of recalcitrants,[17] in line with Apache custom whereby a leader might retain his function only as long as he was successful and therefore popular.

Juh's extended leadership was the more impressive in view of his speech impediment, so severe that he could "hardly talk at all when he became excited,"[18] and Geronimo or someone else sometimes had to speak for him. The precise nature of this imperfection cannot now be ascertained, but it may have had something to do with a tense, mentally-active quality which guided him in leadership; apparently it did nothing to hinder that capacity, at any rate.

## His Early Encounters

Ace Daklugie, Juh's youngest son, told Eve Ball that
his father was at the Battle of Apache Pass on July 15,
1862. Juh and "Mangas Coloradas, Cochise, Victorio,
Nana, and many other great leaders joined forces to stop
that army coming in from the west," but were driven off
when howitzers were joined to the Infantry in the
battle.[19] Juh's growing renown was suggested by an
1882 military map showing a "Joos Canon" crossing the
Arizona-New Mexico line in the vicinity of San Bernardino Ranch. In one edition of a guidebook, "Jhu's Canyon" is listed at an indefinite site in Cochise County.[20]
The chief was becoming more widely known. Yet because
of "the attrition and pressures of constant warfare" Juh
and his Nednais had identified more and more closely
with the Chiricahaus and Bedonkohes on the Chiricahua
Reservation in southeastern Arizona,[21] their inveterate
raiding and plundering threatening to bring punishment
as often upon their hosts as themselves.

When Chochise complained, as he often did, that his
young men were uncontrollable and scurried off raiding
into Mexico, there is little doubt that they went with Juh,
lured to hostile trails by the Nednai and the promise of
easy loot.[22] Cochise, as he aged, became sort of an elder
statesman among the Chiricahuas, and it fell to Juh's lot
to become their war leader.

## The Cushing Episode

In all probability it was Juh who defeated and slew
First Lieutenant Howard Bass Cushing of the 3rd Cavalry, May 5, 1871, south of the Whetstone Mountains.[23]
Cushing, of a family whose members had come to national prominence during the Civil War through extraor-
dinary bravery, was himself an intrepid, somewhat
foolhardy man of great energy. He had assembled an
outstanding record in Arizona through his relentless
pursuits of hostile Indians. In the spring of 1871 he had

undertaken a long scouting expedition against Apaches in the southeastern portion of Arizona, striking at length a band of hostiles north of Old Camp Wallen, which lay on the Babocomari River, northwest of present-day Fort Huachuca.[24] Sergeant John Mott, who brought out Troop F survivors, graphically reported the scout and fight, and recalled: "The Indians were well handled by their chief, a thick, heavy-set man, who never dismounted from a small brown horse during the fight. They were not noisy or boisterous as Indians generally are, but paid great attention to their chief, whose designs I could guess as he delivered his instructions by gestures."[25]

Writers generally have assumed that it was Cochise whom Cushing fought, but Mott's account makes clear that more likely it was Juh, since Cochise could scarcely be confused with the "thick, heavy-set" individual the sergeant recalled. Support for this deduction comes from Ace Daklugie who, incidentally, was said to resemble his father[27] of whom no photograph is known to exist. Ace insisted all his life that "his father led the force that killed Cushing."[28]

An interesting aspect of Mott's narrative is his emphasis upon the close control and decided discipline the leader exhibited over his men. Surely this was a novel feature in Apache warfare, where even preliminary plans for a fight often were disrupted by some over-eager individual and, once the action commenced, it usually was every man for himself. Victorio, it is true, had some notion of tactics and discipline, and possessed the leadership to enforce the latter, but no other Apache exhibited these to such a degree as did Juh and Mott's report illustrates this fact.

## The Chiricahuas Removal

In June of 1876, Agent John P. Clum, supported militarily by Colonel August V. Kautz, then commanding the Department of Arizona, attempted to remove the

Chiricahuas from their reservation to the San Carlos reserve, farther north. This well-known operation was designed partly in pursuance of a "concentration policy" of the Washington Indian Office in order to deal better and more economically with the several tribes, and in part to correct a situation whereby these warlike Indians were quartered directly upon the Mexico line, facilitating persistent raiding into that country. Upon being informed of the intended removal, the Chiricahuas had a small fight among themselves, but this appeared to be resolved by the elimination of the group opposed to the project. Then, Kautz reported: "Stragglers continued to come in daily. On the 7th [of June] 'Who,' 'Geronimo' and 'Nolgee,' or Ca-ca-ri-za, principal men of the Southern Chiricahuas, came in and agreed to bring in their people on Sunday the 11th. But on the 8th . . . a party of San Carlos scouts . . . discovered evidences that showed that the Southern Chiricahuas were acting in bad faith and had left their camp, having killed their dogs [which by barking might have given them away in their flight] and abandoned many useful articles such as Camp kettles, axes, &c... "[29]

Anticipating that some of the Chiricahuas might attempt to escape the removal operation, Kautz already had stationed Captain George M. Brayton, 8th Infantry, with companies A, D and E, 6th Cavalry, and Company B, Indian Scouts, with Al Sieber, chief of scouts, at Sulphur Springs, west of Apache Pass, and, in the San Simon Valley to the east, Major Charles E. Compton, 6th Cavalry, with Companies C, G, I and M, plus chief of scouts Ebin Stanley and an Apache company. When the flight of Juh and his colleagues became known, Kautz ordered the Brayton command to scout the western reaches of the Chiricahua Mountains southerly to the Mexican border, and Compton to scout similarly down their eastern slopes. Brayton's men had a small skirmish with raiders returning from the south, but Compton failed to intercept the enemy, rejecting Stanley's insistence he was close upon the hostiles and might easily take them. Their tracks showed twenty-five to thirty animals. He presumed they had escaped into Old Mexico, as indeed they had.[30] It is worth noting that this party proved to be considerably larger than Compton thought, and that the pony tracks gave a limited and mistaken notion of their number.[31]

These extended operations, precipitated by the bolt of Juh and his friends, illustrate that he also possessed one indispensable quality of the successful guerrilla leader: he was lucky. Had the commands been reversed, that is, had Compton been assigned to the western slope of the Chiricahuas, and Brayton-Sieber to the eastern, he never would have escaped without a fight that could have proven disastrous. This was not to be, however, and Compton's ineffectualness assured Juh a continued career.

At any rate, Juh, Geronimo and their bands began at once depredating widely, though the full extent of their activity was not known and some of the crimes alleged against them, Kautz believed, "were committed by Mexicans." The border country, in those years, was a lawless place.

On December 2, 1876, James Hughes, who ranched near Camp Crittenden, wired Kautz that Apaches had stolen twenty-one horses. Second Lieutenant John Anthony (Tony) Rucker, 6th Cavalry, was ordered to investigate and left Bowie December 11 with ten men of companies H and L, 6th Cavalry, thirty-four men of Company C, Indian Scouts, and guide Jack Dunn. The detachment picked up the trail near Crittenden, followed the hostiles about two hundred miles easterly, discovered and struck their camp about forty miles south of Ralston, New Mexico ( later Shakespeare, near Lordsburg) in the Leitendorf Hills, now the Pyramid Mountains. After a sharp two-hour engagement "the hostile Indians fled in every direction." The "bodies of 10 hostile Indians were found dead, and from the indications observed there was a large number wounded. One Indian boy, about 5 $1/2$ years old, was captured alive near the camp. The boy has since been identified as a nephew of Ger-an-i-mo (the Chiricahua Chief). The hostile camp consisted of lodges containing about 35 warriors.... There is probably a large camp of hostile Chiricahuas somewhere in that vicinity."[32]

No proof exists that Juh was in the attacked camp—nor that Geronimo himself was there, either—except that it obviously was the rancheria of his people, and wherever Geronimo had gone, Juh seemed to lurk nearby. Yet this remarkable scout, from depredation to punishment one of the longest on record in the history of Apacheria, and the circumstances of it, would suggest that Juh indeed may have had a role in it, from first to last. It is probable, however, that because of this action or some other difference, these likeminded cronies split up temporarily, for Geronimo and his associates were heard from next in the spring of 1877 when they were removed with the Mimbres Apaches from southern New Mexico to San Carlos by Agent Clum.[34] Had Juh been present at the time of this removal, because of his growing prominence, he surely would have been mentioned.

## Juh in Mexico

He is not cited in any important way, however, until 1879, and then in Mexico. Thus while Geronimo and such worthies as Gordo, Ponce and a few others, had slipped northeast to the Mimbres Reservation, Juh apparently faded south in late 1876 to his old haunts in Chihuahua and Sonora.

Whatever his activities there, he abruptly reappeared in July, 1879, at Casas Grandes with about forty warriors and fifty women and children, according to a report made by U.S. Consul Louis H. Scott at Chihuahua. Juh, he revealed, had "sent a commission to Gov. [Angel] Trias [Ochoa] asking for peace. Gov. Trias had no force to fight them and had to grant their request. Juh it seems had had a taste of U.S. reservation life and rather liked it and soon demanded food and clothing of the Governor. The Governor called a meeting of the merchants and stated the case to them saying their demands are out of all reason, but I am powerless as I have no troops. A few hundred dollars was raised and sent to them with some blankets, etc."

Scott said that on about September 15 word had been received that some five hundred American troops and scouts had reached Corralitos, north of Casas Grandes, evidently "after Juh and his band who probably made outlaws of themselves in the U.S. and then sought protection in Mexico. Juh expected to be followed as he told several parties that the Americans would follow him, and a short time since he broke up his camp at Casas Grandes and moved further into the State.... I am sure if the troops would overtake and capture or kill the entire band that there would be nothing [but] rejoicing here.... It is reported that Juh murdered a whole [wagon] train in Arizona. How true it is I cannot say, but if he did not, it was only from a lack of opportunity, as he has a terribly bad reputation."[35]

Although the report of the arrival of U.S. troops in Old Mexico was premature, Juh's boast that he had destroyed a wagon train was probably true, though it occurred in New Mexico, not Arizona. Victorio had broken out for the last time on August 21, 1879,[36] and among the bloody clashes that followed swiftly and inevitably was one near McEver's Ranch, the present-day Lake Valley, New Mexico, of which Major Albert P. Morrow, 9th Cavalry, reported, "We had a five hour fight with all of one hundred Indians. We have ten killed and several wounded. All of our stock is gone...."[37] The Record of Engagements also states that ten "citizens," that is, civilians, were killed in this or related incidents, and that the Apaches "captured all their stock."[38] Thus the civilians may have been freighting for the Army, their train overrun, the teamsters slain and the wagons looted and perhaps burned. Juh is known to have accomplished such feats on other occasions. Such incidents often were attended with considerable cruelty to any whites captured alive.

## Back to the U.S.

Supporting evidence for the sudden appearance of Juh north of the border appears in an assessment from 9th Cavalry regimental adjutant John S. Loud, that Victorio had about forty warriors with him when he broke out but "rumor stated he was joined afterwards by Indians from Mexico" since no other Indians were reported out, and the McEvers Ranch hostiles totaled more than twice those Victorio was known to have.[39]

Juh and Victorio never were close friends, may even have been rivals of a sort, but that did not preclude their operating together on occasion. After all, a fight was a fight, and loot was loot, and there swirled about Victorio for many months all the action along these lines that existed in the southwest. Even if Juh collaborated with his more famous compatriot, he still maintained his independence and that of his band.

## Pursuit Into Mexico

Within a month Juh and his incorrigible followers were back in New Mexico, it appeared, for on October 13 a second wagon train was struck and taken, its eleven teamsters shot or burned while lashed upside down to wheels. This was near Slocum's Ranch, in Magdalen Canyon, on the road from Mesilla to Cummings.[40] Other depredations, probably by Juh, extended to the Rio Grande settlements, resulting in burnings, deaths and generating such confusion that Victorio could slip into Old Mexico. Juh apparently joined him as he plunged southward. This time they were indeed pursued, as rapidly as possible, by Major Morrow and his taut, leathery command, eighty-one soldiers and eighteen Indian scouts. The company identifications were not given in the officer's report, although from internal evidence the command probably included detachments from B, H and part of C companies of the 9th Cavalry, Company A, 6th Cavalry, and Second Lieutenant Charles B. Gatewood's

Company A, Arizona scouts.[41] The scouts already had detected the hostile trail leading southward.

Morrow ordered Gatewood to pursue the trail October 19, following with his command the next day. They camped that night at Beyer's Spring, the only free water in the Florida Mountains, and on the 21st moved to the Tres Hermanas uplift, entering Mexico the next day to camp at Lake Palomas. From here, Morrow thought he detected the faint tracery of a smoke in mountains to the southwest. Gatewood's scouts could find no trace of an enemy camp there, but Morrow remained convinced, moved his command in that direction, searching for himself. He discovered a four-day old camp and "evidence of several wounded." Because the Indians had used up all the water, Morrow's men were forced to make a dry camp. At daylight, October 26, the soldiers moved on three miles, discovering another hostile camp, but no water, and followed the trail into the desert. October 27 was the same, but at sundown scouts brought word that they saw a dust ahead. Morrow advanced and "satisfied myself that it was made by mounted Indians. I sent the scouts to reconnoitre the ground and as soon as it was dark enough to hide my dust, followed. I was anxious to get to the Corralitos River which I knew to be somewhere in the direction in which I was marching . . . (I had no guide who knew the country). My horses and mules were dropping down every mile, for want of water." He had been without that precious substance for nearly three days, working hard in the blistering desert, but still he pressed doggedly on.

## *Troops vs Apaches*

Upon nearing the uplift where he had detected the dust, his scouts raced back with the news that the enemy was fortified on the hills before them. Although Morrow was not positive about it, the enemy was led by Victorio and Juh, the two ablest Apache war leaders of this period, and their combined presence promised him an interesting time. So it proved.

His scouts reported that the hostiles had prepared a trap, so Morrow "immediately turned the head of the column to the left, moved up under cover of the mountain, dismounted and prepared to fight on foot." He had not planned to open the attack until daylight, but "the mules and horses cried so loudly and persistently for water, that our presence was quickly discovered and the moment our Indians reached the crest of the first hill they were fired upon.... We had no trouble in dislodging the enemy from the two hills which they then occupied....; they leaped over the works, across the canon trail, and into the works on the opposite hills; we kept up a lively fire and followed at a run until we commenced to ascend the hill upon which they were fortified.... We had reached within about thirty yards of the top and all exposed in the bright light of a full moon [when] they opened upon us with a rattling volley with slight effect, however, as they fired too high. Three of the scouts were hit, one killed and two wounded. We tried persistently to advance, but could not do it. I then tried to flank the hill and sent Lieut. Gatewood around to the right to attack and the moment he opened fire I was to advance. He succeeded most gallantly in getting up within ten feet of the breastworks and held his ground there until he got out of ammunition. The enemy were in the meantime rolling rocks down upon him during his siege. I tried again and again to take the works in my front, but could not succeed," in part because of natural obstacles. He determined to withdraw.

Gatewood reported that "the Indians seemed to have plenty of ammunition, which they rapidly expended in improved Winchester rifles, for when our line arrived within point blank range, the whole top of the mountain was a fringe of fire flashes.... Nearer and nearer to the top of the ridge approached the flashes from the Springfield carbines [of the scouts], and the reports from the Winchesters above were so frequent as to be almost a continuous roar.... Suddenly the firing ceased; the rumbling and crashing of large stones down the side of the mountain could be distinctly heard; the line had run up against a palisade of solid rock... which had not been noticed because the moon was rising behind the enemy's position and the palisade was hid in shadow...."

Gatewood and half a dozen scouts were ordered to reconnoitre a fresh approach with the hope of flanking the enemy, but they were discovered by the hostiles, not supported by the soldiers and an Apache charge threw them back. At length Morrow became convinced he could not oust the enemy and he withdrew, taking his exhausted command to water, some miles distant.

The interesting features of this action were the skillfully selected defense sites, a trademark of Victorio's genius, the determined and persistent defense of them, a characteristic of both chiefs, and the savage charge against Gatewood's little detachment, which was strictly a quality of Juh's leadership. There was also the aspect that this fight occurred at night, when Apaches normally shunned any combat because of their fear of ghosts, but a dread which Juh, on this and other occasions, caused them to overcome. Therefore this, too, was a mark of Juh's hand.

## Escape and Massacre

Having turned back Morrow and his troopers, Juh, Victorio and perhaps Geronimo and their bands trekked leisurely eastward about one hundred miles to a wishbone-shaped, stony uplift called the Candelaria Range, at whose easternmost extremity passes the high road from El Paso to Chihuahua. On its northern slope is a waterhole, today called Tinaja de Victorio, or Victorio's Well, with good reason, for it was here, under Victorio's guidance, that occurred one of the bloodiest massacres in the Apache wars. Disturbed by a few minor depredations, a party of eighteen Mexicans, dispatched from Carrizal in the south to seek out the raiders and, if possible, punish them, fell into an ambush and were wiped out to a man. When they did not return, another party was sent to solve the mystery, fell into an identical trap, and fifteen more were slain. Remarking that "the scene of the conflict was perfectly horrible," Texas Ranger George W. Baylor Sr., who arrived at the site shortly after the second massacre, added that "the Indians had shown great cunning.... The trail passed a low place between and commanded by, three rocky peaks. The Mexicans were fired upon from one side just as they reached the crest of the mountains; they had evidently dismounted and ran into the rocks on the opposite side, when the Indians began killing the horses that they had tied, and opened fire on them from nearly overhead and a peak out to one side. They were all killed...."[42]

Confirmation that Juh was with Victorio in this celebrated incident was sent the Department of State by the Chihuahua consul, Louis Scott: "Morrow ran Victorio sixty miles this side of the line and fought him at La Laguna Guzman.... About this time or before he was joined by Juh... [though] these two worthy cutthroats have not been able to agree for years and personally are not friends. After their fight with Morrow, they crossed to the Candelaria Mountains, where they got in their terribly bloody work on the Carrizal party."

Earlier Scott had told the Department that "Juh informed a Mexican... that he and his Bucks had just returned and had killed a great many white people and some Negroes.... You can rest assured that the northern part of this State will be crowded with renegade Indians who will sue for peace here, and will do their raiding into the U. States... unless they are exterminated or driven out."[43]

Scott now added that the hostiles then attacked Galeana, driving off sixty to seventy horses and killing two men, attacked San Lorenzo where they killed three more and swept up two hundred additional horses. They also captured "a whole train which they destroyed, killing all the train men... which was probably not less than twelve."

Estimating the total warrior strength of the hostiles at probably not more than one hundred fifty "at the outside," Scott urged a concerted effort against them from both sides of the border. "This thing of one side chasing them across the line, and then in a month have the other side chase them back again, is in my opinion a poor way to fight them," he grumbled.[44] He reported that Juh "does not like to talk or be interviewed, but he has at times told of his exploits," never betraying any particular reservation when the mood to boast struck him.[45]

Following the Candelaria massacres and subsequent depredations, Juh and Geronimo split off from Victorio for the last time, perhaps because they had stolen enough stock to supply their immediate wants, or more likely because of personality clashes and differing temperaments. Or perhaps they were tired of raiding and wanted the relative luxury of reservation life for the winter. At any rate, Juh, Geronimo and about eighty of their followers established a hidden camp at McIntosh Spring in the Guadalupe Mountains, about forty miles east of Camp Rucker on the Arizona-New Mexico line. They sent a runner to San Bernardino where he contacted Captain Harry L. Haskell, aide-de-camp to Colonel Willcox, asking that the colonel "be their friend." Haskell was at San Bernardino in the course of a scout he was conducting with Second Lieutenant Augustus P. Blocksom.

## Negotiation and Settlement

This was too good an opportunity to waste by indecision. Haskell, revealing remarkable courage, went accompanied only by his "interpreter," who may have been Thomas Jeffords, well known to the Chiricahuas, to the hostile camp. The enemy had forbidden him to bring any soldiers. The two sides talked and Haskell returned to San Bernardino while the wild Apaches made up their minds. The next day they again sent word to him, and accompanied by Jeffords and this time also by Archie

McIntosh,[46] a well-known scout, Haskell once more
visited the camp where "a very satisfactory talk" was
had. "The Indians say they have heard that General
Willcox has always treated their people well and they
have come to live at peace, that they shall not go on war-
path nor break out from the agency, that they have not
been with Victoria and do not know where he is...."
Plenty of soft soap and maybe a few white lies might be
useful at this point, Juh and his spokesman, Geronimo,
apparently felt. But they had some "demands," in the
modern parlance, as well: "They want the scout companies withdrawn until they have all come in within a week
or two.... They report more Chiricahuas coming in and
want to rest their animals and await the later arrivals....
They also ask that I remain with them until they are
settled at San Carlos... and they want to be with their
own people at the sub-agency [on the south side of the
Gila River, about sixteen miles east of San Carlos] and
they desire that... Nolgee... visit them while here."[47]
Nolgee already had settled at San Carlos.

Willcox quickly assured the alarmed Mexican consul
at Tucson that "Hoo and his followers... will be kept at
San Carlos, where they can harm neither Americans nor
Mexicans, and like the rest of the Indians on the reservation will be treated friendly as long as they behave themselves and will be used as auxiliaries for the subjugation
of hostile bands along the border."[48] The *Star* explained
that "These Indians belong to Cachise's old tribe—the
worst in the deck. They deny having fought with Victorio
and his band, but own up to having done deviltry under
their own chiefs, Hoo and Geronimo.... We take it that
the people of southern Arizona and Sonora are resting
easier, since the surrender of these 'disturbing ele-
ments.'" [49]

Juh and Geronimo settled in on the huge San Carlos
Reservation and it appeared they might stay there indefi-
nitely. Trader Reuben Wood, who had operated his mer-
cantile establishment there for two years, reported in
late May of 1880 that the bands were "perfectly content

A R I Z O N A    N E W   M E X I C O

● CIBECUE
White Mtns.
SALT RIVER
■ FT. APACHE

● SAN CARLOS
FT.
■ THOMAS ● CLIFTON
GILA RIVER

Black
Mtns.

RIO GRANDE

LAKE VALLEY
(McEver's Ranch)
✕ CEDAR SPRINGS
BATTLE MTN. ✕            ✕ MORROW FIGHT ✕ HATCH
■ FT. GRANT                  Cook's Peak (Santa Barbara)
Graham Mtns.   Doubtful Canyon   ● FT CUMMINGS
TUCSON                        ● LORDSBURG      ● SLOCUM'S RANCH
● WILLCOX        Apache   ● RALSTON    ✕ MAGDALEN CANYON FIGHT
Whetstone        Pass    (Shakespeare) (DEMING)
Mtns.   Dragoon   FT. BOWIE   Pyramid Mtns.           ● MESILLA
FT.         SONOITA Mtns.   Chiricahua   ✕ RUCKER FIGHT  Florida
CRITTENDEN ●             Mtns.              Mtns.        ● EL PASO
● ■ CAMP WALLEN            Animas   Big Hatchet ● LAS PALOMAS
■ FT. HUACHUCA  McIntosh Spr. Peak GRANDES   JUAREZ
Huachuca Mtns.   Guadalupe Mtns.   CASAS   RIO GRANDE
● NOGALES   Int. Boundary   ○ (DOUGLAS)         ✕ FIGHT WITH MORROW
                                    Laguna Guzman
FRONTERAS ●   ✕ ENMEDIO FIGHT
RIO BAVISPE   RIO   JANOS   Laguna   ✕ CANDALARIA
                    Santa   MTNS.
              ✕ FIGHT WITH GARCIA   Maria
                              Laguna
Sierra ● BAVISPE                De Palos
de la ● BACERAC   ● CASAS GRANDES
Madera                ✕ FIGHT WITH MATA ORTIZ
RIO                ● GALEANA
Sierra Madre            ● EL CARMEN
JUH'S
STRONGHOLD

M E X I C O
ROAD
TO
CHIHUAHUA
↓
RIO YAQUI

N
Scale in Miles
SONORA
CHIHUAHUA   0        50        100

Don Bufkin

From the approximate positions of the hostile Apaches, the view here is across Cibecue Creek toward the site where Colonel Eugene Asa Carr and his troops camped (this side of the road, in the middle distance of the picture). -PHOTO BY AUTHOR

with their new home, and instead of being in sympathy with Victorio's band [which was still on the warpath], they exhibit hostile feelings towards them." Jeffords, Woods reported, believed that neither would aid nor encourage the raiders even if Victorio should appear.[50] In September it was suggested that Juh and others might be willing to scout for troops in operations against Victorio, then in Mexico, though nothing came of this, probably because Victorio's star was in swift decline.[51]

## An Uneasy Peace

Victorio was killed at Tres Castillos,[52] and an uneasy peace settled over the southwest, broken now and then by such explosions as the Nana raid. Such tranquility could not last, given the circumstances of antagonistic or at least uncooperative tribes crowded upon a single reservation, questionable rationing and supply systems and the lack of a general purpose or objective for the lives of the held peoples. Ripples of unrest began to be felt in the summer of 1881 from the area of Cibecue Creek, leading to uneasiness on the part of whites concerned with the management of Apache affairs.53 On August 10 San Carlos agent Joseph C. Tiffany wired Colonel Eugene Asa Carr, commanding at Fort Apache, that he had "sent emissaries to Juh-Chatto and Natchets [Nachez] camps to see if they are also disaffected," although with what result is not known.

Whether Juh had any role in the sharp clash on the Cibecue August 30, 1881, is uncertain. He is not listed in the incomplete summary of those presumed involved, the report of the investigation by Captain Harry C. Egbert, 12th Infantry,54 but that does not preclude his having been there. Eve Ball quotes Ace Daklugie to the effect that Juh, Geronimo and others of the Chiricahua-Mimbres were present, but does not specifically state that they took part in the fighting.55 Daklugie remarked to Mrs. Ball that Geronimo, shortly before he died in 1909, "told me that he had never understood why he and Juh could have been influenced" to the extent they were by the medicine man whose incantations had generated the Cibecue trouble.56 Cruse, in a letter to Britton Davis more than forty years later, recalled that "several of Geronimo's (Juh or Whoa was the big chief) and Loco's people happened (?) to be at the Cibecue with the Medicine Man . . . when the fight occurred August 30th, but as soon as it was over rushed back to the sub agency at San Carlos."57 With the death of Victorio, Loco had become or remained the principal chief of the remaining Mimbres, now living on the San Carlos Reservation in close proximity to the Chiricahuas.

Regardless of whether Juh had any significant role at Cibecue, he was caught up in its aftermath, and the long sequence of hostilities it let loose swept him toward the climax of his spectacular career. Part of the reason may lie in the abrupt flooding of Arizona with troops in the wake of the fight, ostensibly to thwart any general uprising among the Apaches. By autumn twenty-three troops, companies and batteries, in addition to units normally assigned to Arizona, had been brought in to trample about the zone of unrest,[58] and instead of quieting the situation this may have caused the excitable Chiricahuas to bolt, as former Agent John Clum charged.[59]

## Turmoil and Explosion

Partly because of the superabundance of troops, and partly because the whites did not understand all that had gone on and who was guilty of what, turmoil on the huge reservation continued for the month of September[60] culminating in an abortive attempt to take into custody two small bands of recalcitrants, a White Mountain party of twenty-six under a leader named George, and a six man Chiricahua group under Bonito. This precipitated a thunderbolt explosion of the Juh-Geronimo Southern Chiricahuas from San Carlos toward Mexico.[61] For two years Juh had lived more or less tranquilly upon the reservation, but he would do so no more while he lived. One report suggests that the Juh-Geronimo bands sought to force Loco and Nana at this time to escape with them, but Loco held back[62] and there was no time for debate. They fled, but they remembered Loco and his people. They would return.

Carr, now at San Carlos, received a message on October 1: "[Ezra] Hoag, at sub agency reports that George and Bonito left with their bands last night, probably towards old home and that Chiricahuas broke and went south. You will at once use your command in the most vigorous pursuit."[63] Carr, who detested his superior, Willcox, in any circumstances, must have smiled grimly at the order. He had never approved "giving these red-handed murderers an asylum in the United States," and considered it a "great mistake" to bring them out of Mexico as "almost conquerors, not as captives."[64] This affair, he would have believed, proved him right. But the problem now was to capture or destroy them before they reached sanctuary.

## Pursuit of Juh

Willcox ordered two companies of the 6th Cavalry under First Lieutenant Gilbert E. Overton, and two companies of the 1st Cavalry under Major George Sanford, to pursue the fleeing hostiles, with Sanford in overall command. Colonel Ranald Mackenzie, who had been placed in charge of field operations following the Cibecue affair, confirmed the order.[65] However, Sanford fell ill of his recurring malaria, and Captain Reuben F. Bernard, 1st Cavalry, a veteran soldier and important figure in the Bascom-Cochise confrontation twenty years earlier, came into effective command. The four companies plunged down the trail of the hurrying Apaches toward Cedar Springs, between Camp Thomas and Fort Grant, but the fugitives reached there first. They slew a telegraph operator and four military linemen. Then, spotting an approaching train of freight wagons, they swarmed to the attack a mile east of Cedar Springs, slaughtering six teamsters, as many mules, and looted the wagons, mainly of foodstuffs.[66]

The soldiers, however, caught up with the hostiles while they dallied, and the pursuit became more intense. Bernard reported:

> A steady trot was taken up. As the Indians were going towards Grant, where Lt. Overton's family was, he became very anxious and asked permission to go ahead at a quicker gait; this being granted, Overton's Battalion [that is, the two 6th Cavalry companies] had just gotten in the advance, and was moving at a gallop, when they came on some dead men. Slackening his gait to see who the dead men were, the Indians opened fire from Overton's front and left, the indians being in a strong place in the rocks and timber. Overton at once dismounted and

moved his Battalion towards the Indians' position.

I at once deployed my company [Company G, 1st Cavalry] to the left, mounted, moving well to the left, driving the indians from a hill, then moved to the right front into line as skirmishers, which brought Overton's Battalion on my right, when all advanced driving the indians well into the mountains. It was now getting dark, and the Indians having a very strong position in Mount Graham, I established the skirmish line in as strong a position as I could get, and held it, though the Indians kept up a heavy fire, until about nine o'clock at night.

About eight at night, the indians made a charge on the left of the line coming within a few yards of it. A heavy fire was kept up for a few minutes, when the indians withdrew... The indians got away by going high up on the mountain and passing by and about two miles from, our right flank...[67]

Bernard's losses were a sergeant killed, three men wounded, and fifteen horses killed or wounded.

The directing hand of Juh may be detected throughout this engagement, as reported by the officer. No matter how ingrained the Apache fear of the dark and ghosts, the pragmatic Juh obviously shared no such dread, for here he directed a strong counterattack and successful disengagement starting at about eight o'clock on an October night, when it would have been good and dark. Here also the Apaches, usually ill-disciplined as fighters, were directed into a savage charge that, some accounts have said, reached within ten feet of the soldier positions, pinning down the troopers so that the women, children and impedimenta could be safely withdrawn. With foresight, Juh ordered the throats of the camp dogs slit and the light-colored horses slain, in order not to give away the Indian position in the gloom by sound or sight. The hostiles sped southward.

Bernard pushed on down their trail, following the length of the Dragoon Mountains, being joined enroute by Captain Henry Carroll with Companies F and H, 9th Cavalry, from New Mexico. Below the Dragoons, Juh and his party were caught up with once more, "driven into a very strong position... near the South Pass," but during the night they escaped again and entered Mexico southeast of the Chiricahuas.[68] The southwest now could brace for new hostilities indeed! Little could be done to head them off, for the Chiricahuas, now in the Sierra Madre, were safely beyond pursuit.

## *More Negotiations*

During the winter Juh "kept sending emissaries to San Carlos to persuade Loco and Nani to join him and bring ammunition," according to one source,[69] and not all such rumors were false. Indian inspector Charles Howard confirmed that messengers arrived bearing threats. "Some were inclined to go" with the hostiles, but the leaders demurred so the couriers departed, muttering as they did so that they would bring back enough force to kidnap their "friends."[70] One report specified a threat to return within forty days to get them,[71] and, if true, the forecast was accurate.

The precise reasons why the hostiles felt a compulsion to force their more sedentary relatives to share their Sierra Madre exile are not clear. They did not wish to add to their strength, as their subsequent activities make clear, nor would they benefit in any other discernible way by the addition to their numbers of hordes of hard-to-feed noncombatants. If those among the hostiles with families on San Carlos merely wished reunion, it would have been far more simple to spirit off a limited number of dependents than to force a mass exodus from the reservation. It may be that the genesis for this movement lay with Ka-ya-ten-nae, successor to Victorio as the most able war leader of the Mimbres. He may have wished to gather his people in the Sonora sanctuary and, if so, his urge appeared to have been contagious. Not only the Mimbres, but the remaining Chiricahuas were to be pushed out on the long trail.

## Escape Into Mexico

This climactic affair in Juh's long and varied career and a unique tribute to his genius and energy, can be summarized objectively only by a single word: *incredible!*  ✳

Imagine the situation: military commanders in Arizona and New Mexico during the winter had become increasingly convinced that some sort of explosion was imminent. They prepared for it as thoroughly as they could.[72] The southwest literally swarmed with troops. Spies had been sent deep into Mexico in an attempt to learn the hostiles' intentions.

Juh not only must slip through this enemy labyrinth for two hundred miles from the border to San Carlos—a relatively simple matter for a handful of Apache warriors—but there, under alert and suspicious eyes, perform the stupendous task of gathering up, not warriors alone, but many hundreds of others, young and old, children and aged, poorly mounted or afoot, imperfectly armed or quite defenseless, and herding this rag-tag horde back through the same troop-scoured maze, over the identical two hundred miles into Mexico where, despite their growing weariness, they must continue to guard against chance encounters with scattered military units all of the way to the Sierra Madre!

Who but an Apache would conceive of such an expedition? What other Apache but Juh would have attempted it? Who else could have brought it off?

Late in March, 1882, reports that the Apaches had drifted out of Sonora and into the vicinity of Janos and Corralitos suggested that they might be preparing for a dash across the border, probably for the reservation.[73] A spy wired Mackenzie from Corralitos that "Ju, Apache Chief, here. Think he will go for San Carlos,"[74] and his surmise was sound. Juh and possibly about sixty of his most trusted followers including Chihuahua, Nachez, Chatto and probably Geronimo, slipped north by way of the Stein's Peak Range toward the Gila, their route discovered by Al Sieber on one of his numerous scouts.[75]

By the time Sieber's success could be made known, however, Juh had entered the San Carlos reserve. On Eagle Creek he visited with Na-ti-o-tish,[76] who had been one of the leaders in the Cibecue fight and remained hostile ever since, but even if he tried Juh could not persuade him to join the Mexico recalcitrants. At Stevens' sheep ranch alone the hostiles killed ten people and left two men to hold several hundred sheep for food for the returning party.[77] The raiders then moved down the Gila toward the sub agency, and swept on toward San Carlos.

Its chief of police, Albert D. Sterling, was alerted by a courageous telegraph operator and with an Indian policeman named Sagotal, rode at once in the direction of the sub-agency, meeting the hostiles head-on. They killed the two officers and then, their plans to raid San Carlos, if they had them, aborted, turned and fell upon the Loco band of mixed Mimbres-Chiricahuas and at rifle point, rumor has it, forced the old chief to lead his people into the upper Gila wilderness on the long road to Mexico.[78] The numbers of Apaches involved in this flight have been estimated variously at from four to seven hundred.[79]

The noncombatants migrated mostly through the breaks north of the river, while Juh's warriors ranged widely, pillaging and depredating to secure food, mounts and weaponry, slaying about forty whites, plundering ranches and freight wagons, keeping alert all the time for the numerous bodies of troops scouring the countryside for them. Betzinez said that none of Loco's people had weapons, although many must have been armed in some way, and "we were filled with gloom and despair."

"It was realized that the band would have to make better time somehow if they wanted to escape into Mexico," recalled Betzinez. Thus, while the people waited, warriors scoured the countryside north along the San Francisco River for horses and mules. During this pause, a girl reached womanhood, Betzinez remembered, and within sound of distant shots marking warrior activ-

From high on the sides of Horseshoe Canyon the Apaches fought off Forsyth's troops, the attackers sweeping up the dry watercourse (in the center of the photograph) but unable to climb the sides in the face of determined resistance. -PHOTO BY AUTHOR

ity, the important and elaborate puberty ceremony was carried out, although considerably shortened from the normal four-day affair.[80] So strong was the hold of ritual upon these remarkable people!

With many of the Apaches mounted, the march gained momentum, curved southeast from the Gila through the Peloncillos, the band camping for a night in Old Horseshoe Canyon, just north of Doubtful Canyon. Here the hostiles ambushed a patrol, killing four scouts, but bringing down upon the horde a considerable force under command of Lieutenant Colonel George A. Forsyth, 4th Cavalry, including companies C, F, G, H and M, and Indian scouts. The engagement, though sharp, ended indecisively. The Apaches suffered half a

Photograph taken from the spring before Enmedio Mountain. In the distance is the rocky hill from which Juh, Loco and their people fought off Tupper and Rafferty's troopers and scouts.-PHOTO BY AUTHOR

dozen casualties, including one killed, and the troops six killed, including the four
scouts, and four wounded, an officer among them. The troops then withdrew toward the Gila, and the horde over the mountain to Doubtful Canyon, thus gaining the San Simon Valley, and crossing the Animas or Guadalupe mountains to reach what they believed to be the sanctuary of Old Mexico. They camped at a spring on the west side of Enmedio Mountain. So far the movement had been a tactical miracle, master-minded and engineered by Juh, a classic example of his consummate skill, sense of discipline, energy and bulldog determination.

Betzinez pointed out that "jealousy between different

chiefs and bands" was one cause of dissension when
Apache groups were prowling, one leader often vying
against or attempting to take over from another. "Frequently in such disputes a chief or an influential man
acted as a peacemaker, probably someone who had more
common sense than the hot heads.... But on this occasion [the exodus from San Carlos] no such unpleasant-
ness arose,"[81] and the reason could only have been the
leadership of Juh and the respect accorded him. At some
point Juh and his immediate followers evidently left the
horde, now deemed safely beyond military pursuit, and
headed straight for the Sierra Madre.

Unsuspected by the hostiles, however, the migration
had been relentlessly pursued by a more determined and
energetic force than the one commanded by Forsyth.
This detachment, Companies G and M, 6th Cavalry, and
scout companies B and D out of San Carlos, was commanded by Captain Tullius C. Tupper, Captain William
C. Rafferty, second in command, and with Sieber as chief
of scouts. Tom Horn apparently accompanied this detachment as one of several packers. The outfit had
picked up the trail where the Chiricahuas had made a
swipe at Galeyville, on the eastern slope of the
Chiricahua Mountains, and followed it stubbornly to
Enmedio Mountain. Here on April 28 the second major
action occurred.

## Another Confrontation

Before dawn Sieber had spied out the situation and
guided the Indian scouts into position on a ridge before
the Enmedio Range and behind the hostiles, who were
gathered about a spring three hundred or more yards
distant. To the south of the spring was a rocky hum-
mock of some size, and when the scouts opened fire the
hostiles sprinted for that hill. Gaining it, they secured
their noncombatants among its rocks, while warriors
took up defensive positions. It was a good site for defense and neither the troops nor the scouts could oust

them, although inflicting some casualties,
among them sixteen or more killed. The troops' losses
were light, but the attempt to exterminate or capture the
enemy failed. Virtually out of ammunition the soldiers
were pulled back. In the darkness the hostiles slipped
out of their stronghold and made their way southerly
about thirty miles to the Janos-Bavispe road, near which
they had their third, and most disastrous, fight, this
time with Mexican troops. Wrote Betzinez:

> When we were within a mile and a half of the
> foothills... the warriors who were our 'advance
> guard' stopped to rest and have a smoke. We passed
> them and kept right on going, strung out in a long,
> irregular column.
>
> When we had gone a few hundred yards we were
> suddenly attacked by Mexican soldiers who came at
> us out of the ravine where they had been concealed.
> The first thing I saw was Mexicans firing at the
> Apache women.... Almost immediately Mexicans
> were right among us all, shooting down women and
> children right and left. Here and there a few Indian
> warriors were trying to protect us while the rest of
> the band were running in all directions. It was a
> dreadful, pitiful sight, one that I will never forget.
> People were falling and bleeding, and dying, on all
> sides of us. Whole families were slaughtered on the
> spot, wholly unable to defend themselves.... Those
> who could run the fastest and the farthest managed
> to escape.

Betzinez gives Geronimo credit for salvaging many, and
protecting them, although he reported that many of the
warriors refused to take any part in the action, even
when able to do so. His account is very difficult to dismiss—or to explain—on this point. Juh, of course, was
no longer with the exodus.

The Mexican forces were commanded by Colonel
Lorenzo Garcia, 6th Mexican Infantry, and included a
unit of the Bavispe Guards, the Sonoran Militia, and a
scouting unit in addition to the regulars. The Mexicans
killed seventy-eight Apaches, eleven of them men, and

lost twenty-two men killed, including three officers, and sixteen wounded, three officers among them, out of their two hundred and fifty man force. In addition to the Apaches slain, between fifteen and thirty of them were taken prisoner. It was a crushing blow to the hostiles, but those who survived eventually gained the security of the Sierra Madre where, together with Juh's Nednai, they were able to assemble up to one hundred and fifty warriors and youths of fighting age, the greatest strength Mexican Apaches had been able to muster in more than a decade.

## Refuge in the Mountains

Betzinez reports that the Apaches under Juh and Geronimo made camp "high in the mountains some thirty miles southwest of Casas Grandes," or in some Sierra Madre range otherwise unidentified, but shortly the camp was moved eastward to the San Miguel River, south of Casas Grandes.

"Our group contained Chiricahuas, Warm Springs [Mimbres], Mescalero, San Carlos, White Mountain, and other Apaches, as well as a few Navajoes and even some Mexican and white boys who had grown up to young manhood among the Indians," he said. "We had two principal leaders, Geronimo and Juh."

Largely because of Geronimo's eagerness for whiskey, it was decided to make a "peace" with the Mexicans at Casas Grandes, and this was done. A several days' drunk ensued, when the Mexicans fell upon those Indians in a stupor and slew ten or twelve of them; the others, including young Jason, made their escape.[82] Perusing the records of Apache-Mexican relations, one is struck by the frequency with which the Indians appeared to succumb to white blandishments for the sake of liquor, and although one must not arbitrarily dismiss Betzinez, perplexity over their falling into the old, old trap remains. "Once again the Indians had fallen victim of their own weakness, the love of strong drink, which has been their ruin," Betzinez sighed. "They never seemed to learn from tragic experience."

Following the Casas Grandes slaughter the band moved back into the mountains, camping on the eastern edge of a great canyon of a tributary to the Yaqui River. Here, Betzinez reported, a difference arose between the leaders and although there were no hard feelings, the company split temporarily. Juh withdrew into the deep mountains; Geronimo embarking upon an extended Sonora raid.[83] While Geronimo was absent, Mexican forces caught up with Juh, and a savage fight developed, one which, in garbled form, may have been reported north of the border: "Mexican troops, eight hundred strong, have surrounded Juh's band of Indians, two hundred and fifty strong. The attack was to take place three days ago," the chief of operations in southeastern Arizona was informed.[84] Whether in this action or another, Juh, according to Betzinez, lured the Mexicans up a zig-zag mountain trail and devastated the command with rolling boulders. "Not many escaped," he reported.[85]

## Another Raid

Reunited at the great canyon, the leaders thereupon decided upon a raid on Galeana, southeast of Casas Grandes. After a four day fire dance, the band laid careful plans centered upon a stony, conical hill just to the south of the ridge of low mountains which here cuts the plains of Casas Grandes from those of Galeana. It was November 13, 1882. Two volunteer decoys stole some horses from near the village, luring mounted Mexicans into pursuit. The hostiles could not have known it, but the leader of the Mexicans, a veteran Indian fighter named Juan Mata Ortiz, had been second in command of the expedition which destroyed Victorio two years earlier, so this was in the nature of revenge, however unplanned to that end it may have been. The decoys drew the Mexicans past hidden warriors who then attacked the pursuers from the rear, while the main body

On this hill (center) about 14 miles north of Galeana, Chihuahua, Juan Mata Ortiz and 21 Mexicans were lured to their deaths by Juh and Geronimo. -PHOTO BY AUTHOR

of hostiles slammed into them from their front. The tactics were sheer Juh.

Mata Ortiz led his men in a pounding gallop up the hill (which today is named for him) where they dismounted and began piling up breastworks of the loose stone littering it. Apaches worked their way up the slopes. "Each Indian rolled ahead of himself a round rock about the size of his head," for protection.

One Mexican broke loose and sped for Galeana. "Let him go!" Geronimo called. "He will tell the rest.... More Mexicans will come to the rescue. In that way we can destroy other soldiers." All the remaining Mexicans, twenty-one men, were slain, including the brave—and imprudent—Juan Mata Ortiz who, it was reported, died last and most cruelly. The Apaches lost two men.[86]

Again the bands split, and once more Juh's band, secluded as it was in its stronghold, was attacked by Mexicans "losing quite a few women and children captured and a number killed and wounded. Chief Juh's wife had been killed and his only daughter seriously wounded. This was hard on the chief though he still had three sons," wrote Betzinez, not quite accurately.[87]

After one more sharp engagement in the vicinity of the great canyon, Juh and several of his people, saddened by the loss of relatives, perhaps, separated from the Geronimo-led Apaches for good, withdrawing into the depths of the great Mother Range. They did not emerge even in the spring of 1883, when Crook, by means of his remarkable expedition, penetrated the Sierra Madre and fought, argued and cajoled the bulk of the hostiles to return once more to San Carlos.[88] Not even to Crook would Juh listen. He would never come in again.

## Death of Juh

Death came prosaically enough to the great warrior and chief, although there remained some controversy about details.

The classic version, as expressed by Cruse: Juh "went to Casas Grandes to get supplies—and got drunk on tequila and mounting his pony rode off to the mountains; on the rough trail he swayed too far, overbalanced the pony and both went over the precipice and Juh's neck was broken."[89] Betzinez supports this version: "Juh got good and drunk. While in this condition he rode his horse along the rim of a bluff, fell over the edge, and was killed.... Whisky brought him down just as it did many other Apaches."[90]

Mrs. Ball heard from Daklugie's lips, however, that Juh probably was not drunk at all, but suffered a heart attack which caused him to tumble into the Rio Casas Grandes, near the community of that name. Ace, she reported, held his head above water pending assistance, but Juh died before help could arrive.[91]

His death occurred September 21,1883, according to research by English student of the Apaches Allen Radbourne, who uncovered a story from the Deming, New Mexico Tribune of uncertain date; Radbourne confirmed its information from other sources.[93] With Juh's death the power of the Apaches to make massive war virtually died, for his successor, Geronimo, never became more than a minor chieftain.

# *REFERENCES*

[1] Gillett M. Griswold, "The Fort Sill Apaches: Their Vital Statistics, Tribal Origins, Antecedents," unpublished manuscript at the Field Artillery Museum, Fort Sill, Oklahoma, 71.

[2] Morris Edward Opler, *An Apache Life-Way: The Economic, Social, and Religious Institutions of the Chiricahua Indians*, (New York, 1965), 2.

[3] Jason Betzinez, *I Fought With Geronimo*, ed. by W.S. Nye (Harrisburg, 1959), 15.

[4] Letters Received, Office of Indian Affairs, 1824-81, roll 582, New Mexico Superintendency 10, W1354, Willcox to Prieto, November 9, 1879; hereafter cited as NM with roll and file number.

[5] John Rope, in Grenville Goodwill Notes, *Western Apache Raiding and Warfare*, ed. by Keith Basso, Tucson, University of Arizona Press, 1971, page 110, 307n31.

[6] Gordon C. Baldwin, *The Warrior Apaches*, (Tucson, 1965), 34.

[7] Reprinted in the *Arizona Daily Star*, April 13, 1883.

[8] Morris E. Opler, "A Chiricahua Apache's Account of the Geronimo Campaign of 1886," *New Mexico Historical Review*, Vol. XIII, No. 4 (October, 1938), 367.

[9] Betzinez, 15.

[10] Griswold, 71.

[11] Opler, *An Apache Life-Way*, 134-39; *Western Apache Raiding and Warfare*, from the notes of Grenville Goodwin, ed. by Keith H. Basso (Tucson, 1971), 13-18.

[12] Betzinez, 19; Griswold, 71.

[13] Not to be confused with Nuevo Casas Grandes, a few miles northeast.

[14] Dan L. Thrapp, *Dateline Fort Bowie: Charles Fletcher Lummis Reports on an Apache War*, Norman, University of Oklahoma Press, 1979, p. 99 and n.

[15] Thomas Cruse, *Apache Days and After* (Caldwell, 1941), 90.

[16] Eve Ball, *In the Days of Victorio: Recollections of a Warm Springs Apache* (Tucson, 1970), 123-25.

[17] Betzinez, 83,122.

[18] James H. McClintock, *Arizona: Prehistoric, Aboriginal, Pioneer, Modern* (3 vols., Chicago, 1916), I, 246.

[19] "Cibicu, An Apache Interpretation," by Eve Ball from interviews with Ace Daklugie, *Troopers West: Military Indian Affairs on the American Frontier*, ed. by Ray Brandes (San Diego, 1970), 123.

[20] Map of Southwestern New Mexico, 1882, prepared under supervision of First Lieutenant Thomas N. Bailey, Record Group 393, Department number 15, Cartographic and Audiovisual Records Division, National Archives and Records Service; Will C. Barnes' Arizona Place Names, rev. and enl. by Byrd H. Granger (Tucson, 1960), 41. The name, whose spelling is repeated in the index, is an obvious misprint for Juh.

[21] Griswold, 71.

[22] See, for example, John G. Bourke, Diary, Vol. I, United States Military Academy Library, West Point, N. Y., 130-32, where Cochise was quoted as confirming these raids on Mexico; New Mexico Indian superintendent L. Edwin Dudley, in June, 1874, visited Cochise and observed the presence on his reservation of the "southern Chiricahuas" from Mexico, while raiding continued into that country almost without cessation.—Microcopy 234, Letters Received, OIA, 1824-81, Arizona Superintendency, 1863-80, roll 10, 1874, D1002 Dudley to Smith, June 30, 1874; E50, Dudley to Elkins, April 14, 1874.

[23] The full story of Cushing's last scout as recounted by John Mott, and a map of it, may be found in Dan L. Thrapp, The Conquest of Apacheria (Norman, 1967), 71-77.

[24] Several field trips into this area have failed to locate definitely the site of this engagement, although the general area in which it occurred is clear.

[25] Thrapp, Conquest, 76.

[26] Arizoniana, Vol. I, No. 3 ( Fall, 1960 ), 2, reprinted from the Weekly Arizonian, September 17, 1870.

[27] Eve Ball to writer, April 4, 1968: "Ace told me that he looked very much like his father..."

[28] Eve Ball to writer, October 5, 1967.

[29] Microcopy 666, LR by Adjutant General's Office (Main Series) 1871-1880, roll 265, 1876, Kautz to AAG, Military Division of the Pacific, June 30, 1876.

[30] Ibid. See attached reports from Brayton, June 30, 1876, and Compton, June 18, 1876, describing their scouts.

31 Microcopy 666, 1005 AGO 1877, Kautz statement to AAG, Division of the Pacific, January 29, 1877. In this Kautz quoted the acting Indian agent at San Carlos as of the opinion that the number escaping removal and still at large "to be about two hundred,including thirty warriors."

32 Ibid, Rucker to Asst. Adjutant, Camp Bowie, January 14, 1877.

33 Ibid, Kautz to AAG, Division of the Pacific.

34 For details of this move, see Dan L. Thrapp, Victorio and the Mimbres Apaches (Norman, 1973).

35 NM roll 577, State 1855, Scott to Seward, September 19,1879.

36 Thrapp, *Victorio*.

37 NM roll 578, W2047, Pope to Townsend, September 18,1879.

38 *Record of Engagements with Hostile Indians Within the Military Division of the Missouri, from 1868 to 1882* (Washington, 1882),92.

39 NM roll 578, W2078, Loud to Pope, September 21, 1879.

40 NM, roll 578, Loud to AAG, Fort Leavenworth, October 14, 1879; Victorio Papers, Record Group 94, AGO, LR 6058-1879, selected documents relating to the activities of the 9th and 10th Cavalry in the campaign against Victorio 1879-1880, 6782-1879, Sheridan to Townsend, October 18,1879; hereafter cited as VP, with file number and year.

41 This fearsome campaign and the hard fight which climaxed it is told in Morrow's report, VP 379, Department of Missouri, 1880, dated November 5, 1879, and more graphically, if at some slight cost in accuracy, by Lieut. C. B. Gatewood, U.S.A., "Campaigning Against Victorio in 1879," *The Great Divide*, no volume or number, April, 1894, 102-104; unless otherwise cited, the description of this operation is based upon these two accounts.

42 VP 277-1880, Baylor to Jones, December 3, 1879. See also NM, roll 577, S2424 with Schurz to Evarts, December 3, 1879; James B. Gillett, *Six Years with the Texas Rangers* (New Haven, 1963), 161-69.

43 Record Group 393, Records of U.S. Army Continental Commands, 1821-1920, Department of Arizona, Misc. papers re Victoria's campaign, roll 36, 3973 DA 1879, Scott to Evarts, November 7, 1879; hereafter cited as MP, plus serial number.

44 MP 232 DA 1880, Scott to Hunter, November 28, 1879.

45 Ibid.

46 Juana Fraser Lyon, "Archie McIntosh, the Scottish Indian Scout," *Journal of Arizona History*, Vol. Vll, No. 3 (Autumn, 1966), 103-22.

47 NM, roll 581, W67-1880, Haskell to AAAG, Prescott, December 14,1879.

48 NM, roll 582, W1354, Willox to Prieto, November 8, 1879; January 31, 1880.

49 January 7, 1880.

50 *Arizona Daily Star*, May 27, 1880.

51 MP 2715, Carr, in the field at Bowie, to AG, Whipple, September 1, 1880.

52 For details of his career, including his death and its aftermath, see Thrapp, *Victorio*.

53 See Dan L. Thrapp, *General Crook and the Sierra Madre Adventure* (Norman, 1972), for a summary and analysis of these developments.

54 Record Group 94, Records of the Adjutant General's Office, Apache Troubles, 1879-1883, 4675 DA 1881, Egbert to AAC, DA, Fort Whipple, December 10, 1881; hereafter cited as AT plus serial number.

55 Ball, "Cibicu, an Apache Interpretation," op. cit., 128-30.

56 Ibid, 128-29.

57 Cruse to Davis, October 8, 1927.

58 See Thrapp, Crook, 36-39, for details of this concentration.

59 John Philip Clum, "Apache Misrule," *New Mexico Historical Review*, Vol. V, No. 2, 3 (April, July, 1930), 140-41; 221-39.

60 For a description and analysis of this, see Thrapp, *Crook*, 39-47.

61 Ibid, 48-49.

62 Cruse to Davis, October 8, 1927.

63 AT 1589 WD 1883, Arnold to Carr, October 1, 1881.

64 AT 970 AGO 1883, Carr to General of the Army, April 6, 1882.

65 AT 5843 AGO 1883 Mackenzie to AAG, Department of Arizona, October 15, 1881; Sanford to AAAG, Willcox, October 18, 1881.

66 Details of this pursuit and related events were reported by Bernard, AT 5843 AGO 1881, Bernard to AAG, Department of Arizona, October 14, 1881. See also W. H. Carter, *From Yorktown to Santiago with the Sixth Cavalry* (Baltimore, 1900), 224; *Arizona Daily Star*, October 7, 1881, etc.

67 Bernard Report, Op. cit.

68 Ibid.

69 Cruse to Davis, October 8, 1927.

70 Record group 98, Letters Sent, Department of Arizona, roll 3, 378 DA 1882, Benjamin to Perry, February 19, 1882, with enclosures;hereafter LS with serial number.

71 Frank C. Lockwood, *The Apache Indians* (New York, 1938), 246-47.

72 See Thrapp, *Crook*, for details of this.

73 Record group 393, Letters Sent, District of New Mexico, 1881-1883, 169 DNM 1882, Dorst to Noyes, March 19, 1882; 184 DNM 1882, Mackenzie to Hudson, March 25, 1882; 191 DNM 1882, Mackenzie Fuero, March 28, 1882, are examples.

[74] LS 789 DA 1882, Wilcox to AAG, Military Division of the Pacific, March 26, 1882.

[75] LS 2924 DA 1882, Sieber to Willcox, Whipple Barracks, June 8,1882.

[76] LS 1155 DA 1882 MacGowan to C.O., Fort Apache, included in Willcox to AAG, Military Division of the Pacific, April 27, 1882.

[77] LS 1058 DA 1882 Scully to AAG, Whipple Barracks, April 20, 1882.

[78] Thrapp, *Crook*, 76-77; Jason Betzinez to writer, November 10, 1959; LS 966 DA 1882, Benjamin to C.O., Fort Apache, April l9, 1882.

[79] For this exodus and the several fights attendant to it, see Betzinez, 55-75; Dan L. Thrapp, *Al Sieber, Chief of Scouts* 223-43; hereafter cited as Thrapp, Sieber; Thrapp, *Crook*, 77-95; Thrapp, *Conquest*, 235-50; George A. Forsyth, *Thrilling Days in Army Life* (New York, l900), 79-121; Al Sieber, "Military and Indians: Al Seiber Tells What He Knows About the Late War," *Prescott Weekly Courier*, May 27, 1882; Tom Horn, *A Vindication: Life of Tom Horn by Himself* (Denver, 1904), 74-93.

[80] Betzinez, 60-62.

[81] Ibid, 67-68.

[82] Ibid, 77-80.

[83] Ibid, 81-83.

[84] LS 1632, 1634 DA 1882 Thompson to C.O. Scouting operations, Willcox, May 22, 1882.

[85] Betzinez, 91.

[86] Betzinez, 93-56; *Arizona Daily Star*, December 8, 1882; personal inspection of the site.

[87] Betzinez, 99-101. Juh had had three sons by his first wife, Ishkeh, the youngest, Daklugie, born "near Fort Bowie," in about 1872. By a second wife he had a daughter, Jacal. "Some say she was his only daughter. Others say there was also a younger daughter named Cheuleh," according to Griswold. Apparently the second wife was the one here killed, for Griswold said Ish-keh survived. Cheuleh may also have been slain here. Jacal was not killed but severely wounded in the 1882 attack. Army surgeons at San Carlos subsequently amputated her wounded leg and "she recovered, but presumably died from other causes before the Apaches were sent to Florida in 1886," reports Griswold. Juh's older two sons were captured by Mexican cavalry subsequently and "taken to Mexico City, where they died." The youngest, Daklugie, surrendered with Mangus in 1886, and he and Ish-keh were removed east with the other prisoners, Ish-keh dying at Fort Sill in 1897. Daklugie, who studied at Carlisle Indian School, married Ramona Chihuahua, daughter of the chief, in 1898, later removed to the Mescalero Reservation, and died in 1955. Two grandchildren of Juh survive. Griswold, 71-72.

[88] For details and a map of this expedition, see Thrapp, *Crook*.

[89] Cruse to Davis, October 8, 1927.

[90] Betzinez, 122.

[91] Eve Ball, interview with writer, August 15, 1965.

[92] Indian Raids as Reported in *The Silver City Enterprise, Silver City, New Mexico: 1882-1886* (Silver City, 1968), 8.

[93] Allen Radbourne to author, January 2, 1992.